Cage is a thing or a mindset?

Written by

FURQUAN AHMED SIDDIQUE

CAGED

Mind of Woman

Acknowledgements

Anusha Sohail

Editor
Translator
Layout design

Hina Manzoor

Editor

Jaweria Waheed

Editor

CONTENTS

Chapter 1

GOD'S CREATION

Why were thousands of animals, livestock and birds created in the world? It has a purpose. Why the first creation Adam and the second Eve in God's creation?

Let's review this thing today and think why women? What was so special about a woman who was created?

I believe that any man is incomplete without a woman. Thus, from the beginning, the one who is creator of all has taken this into consideration.

No matter how much research has been done and is being done on women, it reflects a different thinking of nature.

She builds and destroys relationships by seeing the love and sincerity she gives to each person. There is no end of stubbornness. But it is not possible to awaken the conscience. This is a creation that every man wish to understand, but the claim to do so will be proved wrong.

If you want to benefit from this creation, then the legal method is marriage. Every law of Islam in this world is considered by science today. Two, three or four marriages can be legally arranged with this creation.

If someone says that without a woman I am living happily, he does not mean. it is not possible. Somewhere or other, he considers a woman as a source of happiness for him who attracts his heart.

Thus, in this way we can know the importance of the Lord's creation and can adopt legitimate ways for the purity of the next generation.

☆

If there was no woman, nothing would have been

What a creation of God it is

If there was no woman

There would be no regret

If there was no woman, there would be no desire

Lover would not have loved the first one

If this creation was not for God

*There would not have been heaven under the
mother's feet*

*There would not have been her greatness in the
Qur'an*

*There would never have been love for her in the
heart*

The world is empty without a woman

The creation of the Lord is visible to all

What a beautiful thing has been made

The love of the fairies has settled in the heart

☆

Chapter 2

A WOMAN'S JOURNEY FROM LOVE TO DEATH

Some girls give every moment of their life to a certain person playing happily across the courtyard, holding the thorax of her youth in someone's lap, she bestows all her joys on one person without caring for her own.

The moments that are for her friends and for her schooling, a stranger who becomes the center of her life, makes every moment of her life a prisoner and attaches it to permission, he also does not want to live without her.

The comfort come to both of them together, there is no moment that can be spent separated from each other.

In the eyes of the world, this relationship seems to be causing problems. Eventually the problems in love begin to arise. Time passed and the heart was not even familiar, fearing the loneliness.

But the heart is relieved by heart. There was a moment when it seemed as if all the colors had faded away. Maybe it was the last day and with time it would pass. Suddenly a message arrives and heart blossomed like a flower in the garden again and then there is a non-stop link.

A few moments on the phone give happiness of the whole world. The series of gifts began and the talk reached the engagement. Years later the marriage was settled.

During this time, great joys and memorable moments were spent together. They started living together in the journey of life.

It would not be wrong to say that one soul resides in two bodies. Supporting each other in every difficult moment with out caring for own self.

A few years passed happily and then people asked when they would have children. There is no difficulty other than that.

Their lives are calm and charming. They have nothing to do with any of the world's grievances. And then one day Allah filled their laps with the addition of a new creation in their lives. And just like that Allah heard the last wish of this silly girl.

One day she wanted to tell something but did not speak because she never wanted to see her companion upset. The joy of the arrival of mercy in their house passed all day long, but after 11 days of her last wish, she passed away from this mortal world.
She slept peacefully leaving her companion alone, leaving a sign of her love.

Today, wherever she is, May she be happy. Her daughter completes her space. She breathes life and keeps unforgettable love fresh in heart.

The voice that gives peace to my life,

May you always be happy wherever you are

May no one forget your love story,

may everyone find a love like you

You are the pride in the eyes of the Lord.

You were mine, you are mine, you are my life

I every moment I spent with you.

Became my reason for living

Chapter 3

WOMAN'S IGNORANCE

If seen in the world there are many ignorant stories around the woman. Sometimes a woman rises, sometimes she falls. Somewhere she is unmatched, somewhere unparalleled. She is the one who makes one's life or set fire to one's life.

The life of a woman is as deep as the water of the oceans and reveal same horrors as the sea.

The woman is ignorant and foolish. If you read the law of Allah to understand this arguments, it also verifies it, Never can a woman be equal to a man, whether it is a division of property or a testimony. Men are always ahead in the eyes of Allah.

If you consider it in prayers, the ranks and positions of a woman are always behind the man. Whether it is fasting or pray. There are many arguments about human intelligence about woman.

The woman who dreams of being ahead of a man is very foolish and leaves no benefit in equating him.

Whether it is a Western woman or an Eastern woman, from eternity to eternity, due to her ignorance and lack of intellect, she is immersed in the colors of the world and makes decisions that appears to make her superior to man.

If it is tested in millions of houses, every home with such woman tells the story of an unlived house.

The ignorance of a woman has always lost in front of a man's ego and will always lose. Allah made man to present his chest happily in front of naked swords and skilled in economic problems. It is a proof that he is by nature a great warrior.

A woman or a man can change a habit, but to change the nature is completely different story, it has to be molded so that the house will look like the lively home and the happiness surround it.

The joy of living every moment in the arms of your life partner can be felt while holding the rope of gratitude. So a man can proudly say that even the foolishness of a woman is my joy.

But that is possible only when a woman first accepts every way, every wish, every desire that a man has told her for a few years, without any question and imagines that what he says is in fact true. And in a few years that woman can play the man like a toy with a key.

He becomes indebted to her and considers her his every thing. It would not be wrong to say that he started worshiping her.

Today's middle age women teach young girls some of the foolishness that they inherited from their ancestors at the time of their marriage which proves to be a poisonous bowl for these girls.

A man has never come under the rule of anyone and never will. He is hungry for love and always few moments of love fill the color of syrups in his life.

Increasing ignorance of a woman is one of the main reasons for illicit relationship of a man. Therefore, a women should read books based on character rather than appearance and tie the character of holy spouses to their sleeves because their life was a source of guidance for women.

A few foolishness of a woman

Brings many troubles

I have read thousands of such stories

Began and end with the foolishness of a woman.

A woman regrets her foolishness

Then creates some new and strange stories again

☆

Chapter 4

INCOMPLETE WORLD WITHOUT WOMAN

Incomplete youth, wandering traveler searching for water in the desert. Like fish diving in water, fish is incomplete without water, similarly the story of man is incomplete without woman.

If a man says he is complete without a woman, his eyes depict a woman's reflection around him whenever he raises his eyes.

In western society a woman dressed in her cultural dress fascinate the man in front of her.

Even today thousands of men in the world consider being friends with a woman a great success. Why do those who reach the peak of their youth ruin the future they have left, in the arms of girls? Why do a boy who has no friend which are girls, feel inferior nowadays?

It is also true that no woman can be a man's friend. Every man attract the natural and sexual element in woman. So it is better if the bond between a man and a woman is weighed on the scale of marriage or love.

Every man is like a hunter, waiting for signal to hunt. Thus, the sexual organs of a woman drive the man crazy about her. And they have such a magical effect that in a few moments he goes to such a destination of peace which he gets from nowhere.

Those who have a soft heart, and a woman's desire are actually emotional men who are very bold and fearless. Women are attracted to them too because they have pure hearts and true minds.

While these men are more focused on their business or whatever duties they may be. But most of the time they are their needs. Thus, the woman is present in every gathering, as acquaintances or in their free time they hang out with a few more specific women.

Even men of success and ascension are seen as slaves under the control of a woman. This is the reality of a woman. That is why a woman is necessary.

People say I'm complete

But I'm incomplete without her

She is no other than a woman.

In whose arms I am complete.

Chapter 5

SACRED RELATIONSHIPS WITH WOMEN

Islam is the religion of peace, the way it clarified the position of women, no other religion will show justice like this.

Yes, I believe that some women in our society do not have correct knowledge of religion and consider only the veil as the whole religion. They ignore all other orders of Allah. These woman play a major role in making fun of our religion.
Thus the saying:

"Half knowledge is dangerous."

If you look carefully, at a society the role of women is the most visible in it. But if the value of women is not recognized in the society, people use them like garbage cans. Although she is the most respectable, virtuous and honorable of any society. Like one of the attributes of Allah, she is selfless towards her children, like Allah is selfless towards creation.

A mother, first of all I try to describe this sacred relationship "Mother" her role in every society has different importance.

As far as the Western society is concerned. It will not be wrong to say that they seem to be a highly civilized nation. It will not be wrong to say that the source of the teachings of Islam is learned from the Western society. But some of their actions raise questions in the mind. Are they decent?

Allah gave women the ability to bear children. But the tragedy of this society is that it will be known that who is the mother of the child is, but thousands of children come into the world without the name of the father. There is no legislation about it, they are unable to even consider this process as bad.

If you put scientific research in front, why did woman was created? The best way to take advantage of this creation is marriage.

If medical research is done on the period of 130 days, marriage is the way to go from one man to another man, And today science also confirms that all the laws of Islam are for the good of humanity.

If we take care of a few such sacred relationships, then this society, except for the Believe in one God, the whole religion will be improved.

People ask why children love their mothers and why men love women and women love men.

Mother's nature is the example of love. Mother and child's love is selfless, child is a part of mother's body. Mother no matter in any amount of suffering, does not express it.

Similarly, it is one of our first duties to respect and take care of a daughter born from a mother's womb. Major countries in the world are taking various measures to prevent the growth and population of developing countries.

Do they not see the importance of relationships? Do they still want to keep a veil over their intellect? Today, why do they act civilized and use these relationships for their few moments of pleasures?

If a father and a daughter were weighed in a scale in this world, the weight would reveal such love that the human mind would not be able to comprehend it. A yard without a daughter is deserted. She is part of father's liver. She plays an important role in the pride and exaltation of the father, their love is eternal.

So a question comes in the heart that is she also not so holy that her honor is trampled by her brother or father?
I believe that a man is a victim of a woman's lust. A woman plays an important role in giving him a few moments of peace and a great capacity for his state of mind but it is also important to take care of these blood relationships.

These relationships are great for every man and all the other women look like a piece of meat to him. Let's pledge today that we will fulfill all our legitimate desires but will not destroy our relationships.

I agree that my words are very harsh, but this is the truth of my heart.

From civilized society, open prostitution is becoming a business profession in which most of the girls are under the control of a feudal lord and capitalist.

These women are given a name but men go capitalist and return capitalist. If we want, we can do a lot for the betterment of the society. All that is needed is good thinking and intentions which is necessary for the help from Allah.

☆

These Relationships are sacred and forever will

Don't target them for your lust.

Don't show them your inferiority,

Hide your manhood from them.

*You were of high character and you will remain of
high character.*

Just adopt these words from your heart.

I said what was in my heart.

Just show its effect in your hear

Chapter 6

TODAY'S WOMAN

The world seems to have moved ahead in the race to become developed, selling its cultural heritage at bargain prices and the tragedy is that immorality and obscenity, which is a very important topic in religion, today has become the disease which is increasing in every man and woman. In earlier days women were the figure of modesty, but today, if you think about it, very few people are safe from it.

Diseases like adultery are becoming common. The school-going generation is ruining itself in some hobby or the other, which has no precedent, and these problems must be reviewed as they are increasing in the world. These problems leads to the destruction of both this world and the hereafter.

A woman stands by the side of a man in every field and it is also true that she is delicate and performs her tasks in a very good manner and learns every upcoming difficulty through education in advance to remove the deficiency in herself so she could not fail to the man.

It would be foolish to forget to mention a woman's talent here, her actions attracts thousands of people with sweet talk and heartwarming speeches.

But when a woman succeeds and achieves her goal, she starts to believe that she does not need a man. She started telling herself to be successful and alone from every circle

If we think that happiness is the path to success and it will increases with the amount of success, it is quite the opposite. In this world successful people do stupid things like suicide.

Today everyone thinks that he is right, the other is on the wrong path, A woman was always known for her modesty and by always maintaining her modesty, she would be blessed with the comforts of life.

The development of mass media has given rise to various diseases in our generation which destroys their entire life like a termite, by their own hands.

Sometimes something unforgettable dominates the mind, what we do for love is completely our fault. They increase the pain levels for us throughout life. Sometimes we even lose our ability to think, so think before taking a step.

Chapter 7

CLOTHING AND WOMAN

Everything has an identity and it is recognized by this identity and if a human being or any living being is unaware of its importance, then it looks like an inanimate object. Thus, clothing is closely related to a woman's existence.

Every woman wears clothes keeping in mind her religious and cultural heritage, but in every religion, women have great value and importance.

Nowadays the western world has reduced the clothes very much. These revealing cloths shows the appearance of the body and many questions arise in terms of their religion and moral take.

The importance of clothing in attracting a male cannot be ignored. The modesty of a woman, her chastity, apparently tells the world the honor of a man in the house. If one looks at the dress of the woman of that house, it will reveal the truth.

Now big industries are engaged in the race of releasing new designs, which model and which country will suet this dress and which country will top in it.

If you study the rules about women's clothing in Islam and researched from a worldly point of view, it will be proved that every law plays an important role in maintaining the safety of woman in the world. Our Prophet (PBUH) guided his women to wear the type of clothing which play an important role in saving the dignity of women.

We need to understand that today there is a need to bring a revolution. Every woman has to understand the reality of her own life and what is necessary for her.

A lot of problems arise because of clothes, so if the value of clothes and the terms about it are fixed, then the honor and reputation of a woman will also increase and she will be freed from the dirty and mean eyes of the world.

She will be far away and will play the role of a woman who makes a place in the heart of others. This woman will never fail and follows the entire religion. Her success is a must.

It is a firm belief that the real woman settles in the heart of any man forever by adorning her clothes and win his heart with eyes.

Chapter 8

WOMEN AND DIVORCE

The knowledge of the world is getting worn out day by day, it is necessary to understand what the purpose of this knowledge is and only after finding it can be estimated what place we have in this society.

Changing relationships in life and a passion for using them can be an unforgettable experience for any intelligent person. It is not wrong to say that the battle of equality comes to the battle of relationship.

It is also not wrong to say that every smiling face does not reflect any prosperous family but is just a picture for the people. It is a drama to fascinate others.

Life is the name of reality and truth, it is the mirror that if the viewer sees with the real eye, then he become aware of himself, otherwise the ruin of the relationship becomes a destiny.

That woman who competes with men or is jealous of someone can not make place in any emotional man's heart. Some men are realistic. They want to highlight their importance to the woman first and they teach them to walk on the path of moderation and consider the authority of a third person in the life of two people as *Shirk*.

These man want to live by solving every problem between the two and it hurts their ego if it does not happens. Because they believed it would never happen, but it does. In this way, the thing that does not come out of the heart becomes a trap in their mind. It is the first step in the girl's divorce, who tells the third person about her husband.

Saying the word divorce out of the mouth is a very unpopular act. Even God does not forgive polytheism.

A woman uses her poor intellect to make friends wth some men around her and loses her real man by saying that you are skeptic.

But a man meets every dirty face in the world, or he himself is guilty. Thus, he uses a cage to protect his beloved possession. The woman finds it very strange and she ignores it, and sometimes the man's blameless accusation ruins the woman's life.

Isn't life is trust of Allah in us?

A FEW FACTS AND WOMEN

- o A woman trusts someone very quickly if that person is her ideal.

- o If a woman is not sure to carry out the relationship till the last breath, then she should think about this in the beginning, how many men spoil their lives permanently. Men should also keep this in mind

- o Remove modesty and loyalty from the heart of woman, then I am unable to understand what a woman is.

- o The main characteristic of a woman is that she always tries to make the wrong right.

- o A woman should know that a man cannot be a friend to any woman she should take responsibility for her own safety.

- o A woman can cross any limit to please a man

- o A woman's dress defines the honor of the man in her house.

- o

- When a woman comes to love, she is not afraid of her honor.

- If a woman comes to cheat, there is no stopping her.

- A woman takes care of her love without fear of society.

- Get into the habit of listening to a woman's words instead of thinking about them.

- A woman bows her head before the honor of mother and father.

- Complimenting a woman makes her very happy and she starts to love you.

- Sacrifice of a few years after marriage gives lifetime peace which women today refuse to give in the name of freedom.

- After completing a few acts of worship, a woman considers herself a good and pious woman of the world.

- A woman causes the destruction of another woman's house.

- A woman's tongue is not sweet but full of backbiting and slander.

o The reason for the breakdown in a woman's relationship is the involvement of a third person in the house, who in the name of peace actually spends his life happily by establishing an ego in the relationship and only lives by spoiling this relationship.

o Every woman of poor intellect wastes her life in comparing her husband with the husband of others

QUESTIONS

I HAVE A FEW QUESTIONS.

1. Life is not happy, but is the concept of not parting till death correct?

2. If neither of them is happy for reasons of coercion and dislike, the other should separate?

3. Isn't along with the training of women, the training of men is also important in the society.

4. What we think of love and get married and get divorced, isn't that really attraction?

5. Lovers never want anyone's loss no matter what. Why is it the opposite here? Thinking like this, then call love is correct?

6. There are many components before a divorce takes place, but the final one becomes the issue on which the decision is made. What are your thoughts?

7. A woman plays an important role in ruining another woman's house. Is this woman's appearance and relationships also very deceptive?

8. Can the children of those who live by making women slaves and prisoners escape from this crime?

9. Isn't lack of tolerance leads to divorce?

10. Not every divorced woman is guilty. Are there mistakes on both sides?

11. Does divorce make life better or cause problems?

www.ingramcontent.com/pod-product-compliance
Lightning Source LLC
Chambersburg PA
CBHW061647130726
47996CB00003B/1501